In memory of
Lieutenant Peter Hines, 3 Platoon, A Company, 6th Battalion, RAR
Corporal John Needs, 3 Platoon, A Company, 6th Battalion, RAR
Warrant Officer Phil Thompson OAM
~JS

In memory of Captain Paddy Young, 6th Battalion, RAR
~CS

# I Was Only Nineteen

*For*
*Denny Schumann (nee Storen)*
*Mick Storen*
*Frank Hunt*
~ John Schumann

The illustrator would like to acknowledge in particular the books of Peter Haran.
The vivid descriptions, and detail, in these firsthand stories was invaluable.

This paperback edition published by Allen & Unwin in 2019

First published by Allen & Unwin in 2014

'I Was Only 19 (A Walk in the Light Green)' by John Schumann © 1983 Universal Music Publishing Pty Ltd.
All rights reserved. International copyright secured. Reprinted with permission.
Copyright © Illustrations, Craig Smith 2014

All rights reserved. No part of this book may be reproduced or transmitted in any form or by any means, electronic or mechanical, including photocopying, recording or by any information storage and retrieval system, without prior permission in writing from the publisher. The Australian *Copyright Act 1968* (the Act) allows a maximum of one chapter or ten per cent of this book, whichever is the greater, to be photocopied by any educational institution for its educational purposes provided that the educational institution (or body that administers it) has given a remuneration notice to the Copyright Agency (Australia) under the Act.

Allen & Unwin
83 Alexander Street
Crows Nest NSW 2065
Australia
Phone: (61 2) 8425 0100
Email: info@allenandunwin.com
Web: www.allenandunwin.com

A catalogue record for this book is available
from the National Library of Australia
catalogue.nla.gov.au

ISBN 978 1 76052 704 4

For teaching resources, explore www.allenandunwin.com/resources/for-teachers

Cover and text design by Sandra Nobes
Set in 20 pt Bauer Bodoni by Sandra Nobes
Colour reproduction by Splitting Image, Clayton, Victoria
Printed in October 2018 by Hang Tai Printing (Guang Dong) Ltd., China.

1 3 5 7 9 10 8 6 4 2

The song 'I Was Only 19' is available through iTunes:
https://itunes.apple.com/au/album/i-was-only-19-single/id632696107
More about John, and the song: www.schumann.com.au/john

# I Was Only Nineteen

Words by John Schumann
Pictures by Craig Smith

ALLEN&UNWIN
SYDNEY · MELBOURNE · AUCKLAND · LONDON

Mum and Dad and Denny saw the passing-out parade at Puckapunyal. (It was a long march from cadets.)

The Sixth Battalion was the next to tour and it was me who drew the card. We did Canungra and Shoalwater before we left.

And Townsville lined the footpath as we marched down to the quay.
This clipping from the paper shows us young and strong and clean.
And there's me in my slouch hat, with my SLR and greens.

God help me, I was only nineteen.

From Vung Tau, riding Chinooks, to the dust at Nui Dat,
I'd been in and out of choppers now for months.
But we made our tents a home, VB and pin-ups on the lockers,
and an Asian orange sunset through the scrub.

God help me, I was only nineteen.

A four-week operation, when each step
could mean your last one on two legs:
it was a war within yourself.

But you wouldn't let your mates down
'til they had you dusted off...

...so you closed your eyes and thought about something else.

Then someone yelled out 'Contact', and the bloke behind me swore.

We hooked in there for hours…

…then a God almighty roar.

Frankie kicked a mine the day that mankind kicked the moon.

God help me, he was going home in June.

I can still see Frankie,
drinking tinnies in the Grand Hotel
on a thirty-six hour rec leave in Vung Tau.

And I can still hear Frankie, lying screaming in the jungle
'til the morphine came and killed the bloody row.

And the Anzac legends didn't mention mud and blood and tears,
and stories that my father told me never seemed quite real.
I caught some pieces in my back that I didn't even feel...
God help me, I was only nineteen.

And can you tell me, doctor, why I still can't get to sleep?
And why the Channel Seven chopper chills me to my feet?
And what's this rash that comes and goes – can you tell me what it means?

God help me, I was only nineteen.

G'day,

In 1968, I was in high school and the Vietnam War was in full swing.
Lots of young Australian men were being shipped off to Asia. My mum was
really frightened that, in a few years, I would have to join them.

Not everyone agreed that Australia should be fighting in this war.
Pretty soon, thousands of people were marching through Australian cities
and towns to demonstrate against it.

By January 1973, Australia had pulled all its forces out of Vietnam.
But our servicemen and women weren't welcomed home like Australians had
been from earlier wars, and I remember feeling very sorry for them.
They'd come back sick and injured from an unpopular war and it seemed
like the rest of us didn't want to know.

In 1981, I met Denny, my future wife. Her brother, Mick, had fought
in Vietnam, and in 1969 he'd been involved in a very serious land-mine
incident in the Long Hai Hills.

After Mick and I got to be mates, I told him I'd always wanted to
write a song about the Australians who fought in Vietnam. I asked him
if he would tell me his story. He agreed, and one night we recorded
a long, long conversation about his year there. I reckon I listened
to that recording a hundred times or more.

Sometimes songs take months to write. Sometimes they just tumble out.
When I actually sat down to write 'I Was Only 19', it took me fifteen
minutes. It was that quick.

'I Was Only 19' has received a lot of praise from veterans. Perhaps
this is because the song reminds us that we can oppose a war vigorously
but we must always support the people we send to fight it.

In lots of ways, '19' changed my life. Because of this song, I've met
some wonderful people, I've been to some amazing places and I've done some
amazing things. But the greatest pleasure I get is when I'm recognised
out of the blue by veterans and their families and thanked so warmly and
genuinely. I have a lot of veteran mates now, and they are always there
for me when it feels like the wind's blowing in the wrong direction.

Thirty years later, it's important to remember the courage and trust
Mick showed when he stepped outside the closed circle of Vietnam veterans
to tell me his story. We all owe him.

Oh, and one last thing — don't let anyone ever tell you that songs
can't change the world.